DSCR Risk Management

How to Use Leverage Without Blowing Up Your Portfolio

By Joseph G. Correa

Licensed Mortgage Broker, Finibi Mortgage

Copyright & Legal Notice

Published by Live Stronger Faster

First Edition, 2026

Table of Contents

Introduction

Leverage is the most powerful wealth-building tool in real estate, and it is also the fastest way to lose everything when it is misunderstood. DSCR loans allow investors to scale faster than any financing method in history because they remove personal income from the approval equation and replace it with property cash flow. That freedom is what allows investors to build large rental portfolios, acquire multiple properties at once, and operate like professional asset managers instead of wage-based borrowers. However, that same freedom introduces a new category of risk that most investors are never taught to manage. This book exists because DSCR loans are not dangerous, but unmanaged leverage is, and the majority of investors using DSCR today have no formal framework for risk control, liquidity protection, or portfolio stress testing.

Most real estate losses do not happen because investors buy bad properties. They happen because investors become over-leveraged without realizing it. When rents flatten, interest rates adjust, insurance rises, taxes increase, or vacancy stretches longer than expected, small negative changes compound rapidly when a portfolio is built on high leverage. DSCR loans are not fragile, but they are unforgiving to sloppy underwriting, weak reserves, and unrealistic assumptions. Investors who understand risk management can hold DSCR portfolios through recessions, rate cycles, and market corrections while continuing to grow. Investors who do not are often forced to sell at the worst possible time, not because the property failed, but because their liquidity and cash flow strategy did.

This book will teach you how to think like a professional real estate risk manager instead of a hopeful property buyer. You will learn how banks and institutional lenders evaluate DSCR portfolios behind the scenes, how they model risk, and how you can use those same frameworks to protect your wealth. You will understand why two investors with identical properties can have completely different financial outcomes depending on how their leverage is structured, how their loans are layered, and how their cash reserves are managed. Risk in DSCR lending is not about fear; it is about math, cash flow, and timing, and once you understand those three variables, you can control your outcome with precision.

A DSCR loan measures the relationship between rental income and debt obligations, but it does not measure how resilient your portfolio is under stress. That is where most investors fail. A portfolio can meet DSCR guidelines and still be fragile if it lacks proper reserve planning, debt stacking discipline, and diversification across property types and markets. This book will show you how to design a DSCR portfolio that survives rent dips, maintenance spikes, insurance hikes, and interest rate changes without forcing you into distressed decisions. The goal is not to eliminate risk. The goal is to make risk predictable, manageable, and profitable.

One of the greatest advantages of DSCR lending is that it allows investors to operate outside the constraints of personal debt-to-income ratios. That means you can keep buying even when your W-2 income is low, your tax returns show heavy depreciation, or your businesses are reinvesting profits. But that also means you are now responsible for managing risk the way a bank would. When your income is no longer the safety net, your portfolio structure becomes the safety net. That is why this book will focus on portfolio-level risk instead of property-level risk. You are not just buying houses. You are building a financial system that must remain solvent across years, not just months.

In this introduction, you will learn how DSCR risk is created, how it compounds, and how it can be controlled. You will understand why the most dangerous DSCR portfolios are often the ones that appear the most profitable on paper. High cash-on-cash returns, aggressive leverage, and fast scaling can mask structural weakness that only becomes visible when the market shifts. By the time most investors realize their portfolio is fragile, it is already too late. This book gives you the tools to see those problems before they happen. Risk management in DSCR lending is about three pillars: cash flow stability, liquidity, and debt structure. Cash flow stability means your rents can absorb shocks without breaking. Liquidity means you have access to capital when problems arise. Debt structure means your loans are layered in a way that gives you flexibility instead of trapping you. When these three pillars are aligned, you can hold properties through downturns, refinance when conditions improve, and continue acquiring assets while other investors are forced to exit.

This book is written for investors who want to build real wealth, not fragile paper portfolios. Whether you own two rentals or twenty, the same risk principles apply. In fact, the larger your portfolio becomes, the more critical risk management becomes. A single vacancy means nothing in a five-property portfolio, but in a highly leveraged ten-property portfolio with thin margins, it can create a chain reaction that affects every loan. You will learn how to design your portfolio so that no single property can put the entire system at risk.

As a licensed mortgage broker who works with DSCR loans every day, I see both sides of this market. I see investors who grow steadily, refinance safely, and build long-term wealth, and I see investors who move too fast, take on too much leverage, and get forced out when conditions change. The difference is not intelligence or ambition. It is structure. This book gives you the structure that banks, hedge funds, and institutional landlords use, adapted for individual investors who want to play at a professional level.

DSCR loans are not meant to be used recklessly. They are meant to be used strategically. When you understand how to manage risk, you can use DSCR financing to build a portfolio that grows faster than conventional loans while remaining safer than most people believe possible. You will learn how to stress test your rentals, how to calculate your true break-even point, how to build reserves that actually protect you, and how to avoid stacking risk across multiple loans and properties.

By the time you finish this book, you will no longer think about DSCR loans as simple rental mortgages. You will see them as components of a financial system that you control. You will know how much risk you are taking, how much downside you can survive, and how much upside you can safely pursue. That clarity is what separates professional investors from gamblers.

The goal of this book is not to make you conservative. The goal is to make you precise. When you know exactly how your leverage works, how your cash flow behaves under pressure, and how your debt interacts across properties, you can grow faster with less fear. Risk does not disappear when you ignore it. It multiplies. But when you manage it correctly, it becomes the engine that powers long-term wealth.

This is the missing piece of DSCR education. Most books teach you how to get approved. This book teaches you how to stay in the game. In the chapters that follow, you will learn how to protect what you build, how to grow without overexposing yourself, and how to turn DSCR leverage into a sustainable wealth engine that works for decades, not just deal by deal.

Chapter 1

Understanding DSCR Risk at the Portfolio Level

Risk in DSCR investing is not created by the loan itself, but by how that loan interacts with cash flow, expenses, interest rates, and the rest of your portfolio. Most investors think risk comes from buying the wrong property, but in reality most DSCR portfolio failures come from stacking too much debt against too little margin. DSCR loans allow you to qualify based on property income instead of personal income, which is incredibly powerful, but it also means the property must carry the full financial burden of the loan without the safety net of your paycheck. When that burden becomes too heavy, small changes in the market can quickly become major financial problems.

At the individual property level, DSCR looks simple. You divide the rental income by the mortgage payment. If the result is above the lender's minimum, usually between 1.00 and 1.25, the loan is approved. But that calculation hides a dangerous truth. It only measures whether the property can pay the mortgage today. It does not measure whether the property can survive higher insurance, higher taxes, unexpected repairs, vacancy, or future rate adjustments. When investors build portfolios by repeating that same minimum DSCR approval over and over, they create a fragile structure that only works if nothing ever goes wrong.

Portfolio-level risk is what happens when multiple properties all depend on the same assumptions. If rents drop by ten percent across a market, every DSCR loan in that city becomes weaker at the same time. If insurance premiums double or property taxes increase, your entire portfolio feels it all at once. That is why risk must be evaluated across all properties, not one loan at a time. A portfolio with ten DSCR loans at a 1.05 ratio is far more dangerous than a portfolio with five loans at 1.40, even if the total value is the same. The first portfolio has no breathing room. The second can absorb shocks.

The biggest mistake investors make with DSCR loans is believing that passing the lender's DSCR test means the deal is safe. Lenders only test for loan-level risk. They are not responsible for your personal survival if the market turns. They only care that the property meets their minimum guidelines at the time of closing. That means the burden of risk management falls entirely on the investor. Professional investors never ask, "Will this loan get approved?" They ask, "How much stress can this deal survive before it becomes a problem?"

True DSCR risk management begins by understanding margin. Margin is the difference between what the property earns and what the property must pay. If your property earns $3,000 per month and your mortgage is $2,500, your DSCR might pass at 1.20, but your margin is only $500. That $500 must cover vacancy, maintenance, property management, insurance increases, tax increases, and any unexpected repairs. If one of those expenses rises by $400, the property is suddenly very close to failure. If two happen at the same time, you are in trouble.

Now expand that across a portfolio. If you own eight properties that each only have $400 to $600 of monthly margin, a single market shift can wipe out thousands of dollars in cash flow overnight. That is how investors end up needing to inject personal money just to keep loans current. The portfolio might still technically meet DSCR, but the investor is no longer financially stable. That is what blowing up looks like in slow motion.

Another hidden risk in DSCR portfolios is correlation. Correlation means how much one property's performance is connected to another's. If all your rentals are in the same city, rent cycle, insurance market, and tax jurisdiction, then their risks are highly correlated. When one property suffers, they all suffer. A professional DSCR investor spreads risk across property types, locations, and tenant profiles so that not all properties move together. This makes the portfolio far more resilient.

Interest rate risk is also magnified in DSCR lending. Many DSCR loans use adjustable rates or short-term fixed periods. That means a loan that works today at 7 percent might reset to 9 or 10 percent in the future. A higher interest rate increases the monthly payment, which lowers DSCR. Investors who do not model rate changes are gambling on the future. Risk management means knowing exactly how high rates can rise before your portfolio breaks.

Liquidity risk is just as important as cash flow risk. Liquidity means having access to money when something goes wrong. Even the best DSCR portfolio will face vacancies, repairs, and surprises. Investors who rely on thin margins and no reserves are one bad month away from distress. Professional DSCR portfolios always include cash reserves, lines of credit, or other capital buffers that can carry the portfolio through rough periods.

The final layer of DSCR risk is leverage stacking. This happens when investors use one property to fund another, which then funds another, creating a chain of dependencies. When everything goes well, this accelerates growth. When something breaks, it causes a domino effect. A safe portfolio uses leverage strategically, not recklessly. Each loan must be able to stand on its own without depending on another property's performance to survive.

DSCR risk management is not about fear. It is about control. When you know how much margin you have, how much shock your portfolio can absorb, and how your loans interact, you stop guessing and start managing. This is what allows you to scale faster than conventional investors while remaining financially secure.

How DSCR Risk Builds in a Real Portfolio

Imagine an investor owns four rental properties, each purchased using DSCR loans. Each property rents for $2,500 per month. Each mortgage payment is $2,000 per month. That gives each property a DSCR of 1.25 because $2,500 divided by $2,000 equals 1.25. On paper, all four loans are strong and fully compliant with lender guidelines. The investor feels confident and begins to plan for more purchases.

Now let's look at real numbers beyond DSCR. Each property also has $300 in property taxes, $200 in insurance, $150 in maintenance, and $150 in property management. That adds $800 in non-mortgage expenses. So the true monthly cost of each property is $2,000 for the loan plus $800 for expenses, which equals $2,800. But the rent is only $2,500. That means each property is actually losing $300 per month even though the DSCR looks healthy. Multiply that by four properties and the investor is losing $1,200 per month without realizing it.

Now assume the investor self-manages and removes the $150 management cost. That brings expenses down to $650 and total cost to $2,650. With rent of $2,500, the loss is now $150 per property, or $600 per month across the portfolio. The investor is still feeding the portfolio out of pocket.

Next, assume rents increase to $2,700. Now income is $2,700 and expenses are $2,650, so each property earns $50 per month. Across four properties, that is $200 per month. That looks positive, but the margin is extremely thin. A single $500 repair wipes out two and a half months of profit for one property. If two properties need repairs, the portfolio goes negative.

Now imagine insurance rises by $100 per month on each property. That increases expenses to $2,750. With rent still at $2,700, each property loses $50. Across four properties, that is a $200 monthly loss. Nothing changed about the DSCR on paper, but the portfolio is now bleeding cash.

Now consider interest rate risk. Suppose these are adjustable DSCR loans and rates rise enough to increase each mortgage by $300 per month. The new mortgage is $2,300. Expenses become $2,300 plus $750 for taxes, insurance, and maintenance, totaling $3,050. With rent at $2,700, each property loses $350. Across four properties, the investor is losing $1,400 per month.

This is how portfolios fail. Not all at once, but through compounding pressure. The investor may try to hold on using savings or credit cards, but eventually liquidity runs out. Even though the properties technically met DSCR when purchased, the lack of margin and reserves made the portfolio fragile.

Now let's compare this to a safer portfolio. Imagine four properties each renting for $3,000 instead of $2,500. Mortgage payments are still $2,000. Taxes, insurance, and maintenance are still $800. Total cost is $2,800. That leaves $200 of true cash flow per property. Across four properties, that is $800 per month.

If insurance rises by $100, expenses become $2,900 and cash flow becomes $100 per property, or $400 total. The portfolio is still positive. If rates rise and mortgages increase by $300, total cost becomes $3,200, which exceeds rent by $200, but the investor has reserves built from months of positive cash flow and can survive until rents catch up.

The difference between these two portfolios is not DSCR

approval. It is margin, liquidity, and structure. One portfolio looks good on paper but collapses under pressure. The other bends but does not break.

This is the heart of DSCR risk management. You are not managing one loan. You are managing a system of cash flows, expenses, and leverage. When you understand how the math really works, you can build a DSCR portfolio that grows fast and survives anything the market throws at it.

Chapter 2

Cash Flow Buffers, Reserves, and Survival Capital

Most investors believe that if their rental properties show positive cash flow, they are financially safe. In reality, cash flow alone does not keep DSCR portfolios alive. What protects investors is buffer capital. Buffer capital is the difference between being profitable on paper and being able to survive when real life hits. DSCR loans remove personal income from underwriting, which means the investor must replace that safety net with liquidity, reserves, and strategic cash flow management. Without buffers, even profitable portfolios collapse.

Every rental property produces two types of income. The first is operating cash flow, which is what remains after paying the mortgage and expenses. The second is survival cash flow, which is what accumulates in reserves. Survival cash flow is what pays for vacancies, major repairs, insurance spikes, tax increases, and interest rate resets. Most investors focus only on the first type and completely ignore the second. That is why so many DSCR portfolios fail during periods of stress. Professional real estate investors do not ask, "Does this property cash flow?" They ask, "How long can this property survive if it does not?" A DSCR loan might allow a property to qualify at a 1.10 or 1.20 ratio, but that does not guarantee the property can survive a three-month vacancy, a $10,000 roof, or a $3,000 HVAC replacement. Reserves are what turn leverage into a tool instead of a trap.

A proper DSCR reserve system operates at three levels. The first level is property-level reserves. This is money saved for each property to handle its own problems. The second level is portfolio-level reserves, which provide backup if multiple properties are stressed at the same time. The third level is access to capital, which can include HELOCs, business credit lines, or cash accounts that can be deployed quickly. When all three layers exist, the investor is extremely hard to destabilize.

Property-level reserves are the most basic form of protection. Every rental should have enough cash set aside to cover at least three to six months of full operating expenses, including the mortgage. This means if a property costs $3,000 per month to operate, it should have $9,000 to $18,000 in reserves. This money is not profit. It is insurance. It is what allows you to hold through vacancies, evictions, repairs, and seasonal downturns.

Portfolio-level reserves exist because real problems rarely happen one at a time. When a recession hits, multiple tenants may leave. When insurance increases, it increases everywhere. When a hurricane or economic shock occurs, multiple properties need attention simultaneously. Portfolio-level reserves allow you to support weaker properties while they stabilize without draining personal savings or defaulting on loans.

Access to capital is the final layer of defense. This includes HELOCs, business lines of credit, credit cards, or investor capital that can be deployed when reserves are not enough. Smart DSCR investors set up this capital before they need it. Waiting until you are in distress makes financing expensive or impossible. Liquidity must be built in good times so it exists in bad times.

One of the most dangerous mistakes DSCR investors make is using every dollar of cash flow to buy more properties. This creates a portfolio that grows fast but has no shock absorbers. The moment something goes wrong, the investor is forced to choose between paying personal bills and keeping loans current. That is when panic selling, loan defaults, and destroyed credit occur.

Cash flow buffers allow you to scale safely. Instead of using all profits to buy more properties, professional investors allocate a portion to reserves first. Growth is delayed slightly, but survival becomes almost guaranteed. The goal is not to grow as fast as possible. The goal is to grow as fast as you can without ever being forced to sell.

Another critical concept is burn rate. Burn rate is how fast your portfolio consumes cash during a crisis. If your portfolio loses $3,000 per month during a downturn and you have $60,000 in reserves, you have twenty months of survival time. That gives you room to wait for rents to rise, refinance, or sell strategically instead of desperately. Without reserves, the same downturn destroys you in weeks.

DSCR portfolios that survive recessions are not the ones with the highest returns. They are the ones with the strongest buffers. High leverage with no reserves is not investing. It is speculation. Risk management means you assume things will go wrong and you prepare for them financially.

Cash flow buffers also give you negotiating power. When you are not desperate, you can refinance when rates drop, sell when prices are high, and buy when others are forced out. Liquidity turns downturns into opportunities.

This chapter teaches you that cash flow is not just income. It is ammunition. Reserves are not wasted money. They are what allow your DSCR strategy to work over decades instead of collapsing during the first major market shift.

How Reserves Determine Whether a DSCR Portfolio Survives

Assume an investor owns five rental properties, each financed with DSCR loans. Each property rents for $3,000 per month. Each mortgage is $2,200. Taxes, insurance, maintenance, and management average $600 per month. That means each property costs $2,800 to operate and produces $200 of cash flow. Across five properties, that is $1,000 per month.

Now assume the investor uses all $1,000 to make down payments on new properties. There are no reserves. On paper, everything looks good. But then two tenants leave at the same time. Those two properties now produce $0 in rent but still cost $2,800 each to operate. That is $5,600 of negative cash flow. The remaining three properties still earn $600 total. That means the portfolio is now losing $5,000 per month.

If the investor has no reserves, they must cover that $5,000 from personal savings or credit. If this lasts three months, they need $15,000. If one tenant damages a unit and requires $8,000 of repairs, the total needed becomes $23,000. Most investors do not have this.

Now compare this to a buffered investor. Before buying five properties, the investor built property-level reserves of $15,000 per property, totaling $75,000. They also have a $50,000 HELOC. When two tenants leave, the investor pulls

$5,600 per month from reserves. After three months, $16,800 has been used. The $8,000 repair is also paid. Total used is $24,800. The investor still has over $50,000 left.

Because they were not desperate, they could renovate, re-rent, and raise rents. After four months, both units are rented again at $3,200. Now each of those properties produces $400 instead of $200. The portfolio cash flow rises to $1,400 per month. That extra $400 is now used to rebuild reserves.

The difference between the two investors was not luck. It was preparation. The first investor had positive cash flow but no survival capital. The second had buffers and control. That is how DSCR portfolios survive stress and come out stronger.

Chapter 3

Interest Rate, Loan Structure, and Refinance Risk

DSCR loans give investors a powerful advantage because they are underwritten on property cash flow instead of personal income, but this same structure introduces one of the largest hidden risks in real estate: payment volatility. Unlike many traditional mortgages that lock in fixed rates for thirty years, DSCR loans often use short fixed periods, adjustable rates, or interest-only structures. These loan features increase short-term cash flow and approval odds, but they also expose investors to future payment shocks that can destabilize even strong portfolios if not properly managed.

Most DSCR investors focus on the payment they have today instead of the payment they might have in the future. This is one of the most dangerous mistakes in leverage-based investing. When interest rates rise, DSCR declines. When DSCR declines, refinancing becomes harder. When refinancing becomes harder, investors get trapped in loans they can no longer afford. This is called refinance risk, and it is the number one reason DSCR portfolios fail after periods of rapid growth. Loan structure determines how much time you have before risk arrives. A five-year fixed DSCR loan means your payment is stable for five years. A three-year fixed means risk arrives sooner. An adjustable loan means risk is always present. A portfolio with multiple loans resetting in the same year creates a time bomb. If market conditions are unfavorable when those resets occur, the entire portfolio can be pushed into distress at once.

Professional DSCR investors do not guess about interest rates. They model them. Before taking a loan, they calculate how high the payment can go before the property becomes cash-flow negative. They also calculate how high rates can rise before DSCR falls below refinance thresholds. This allows them to know in advance whether a deal is safe or fragile.

Interest-only DSCR loans are another powerful but dangerous tool. These loans lower payments during the interest-only period, making DSCR appear stronger and cash flow higher. But when principal payments begin, the payment jumps. Investors who do not plan for this increase find themselves with properties that no longer qualify for refinancing or produce positive cash flow.

Refinancing is not guaranteed. It depends on DSCR, loan-to-value, interest rates, and market conditions. Investors who assume they will always be able to refinance are building portfolios on hope instead of math. Risk management means structuring loans so that refinancing is optional, not required for survival.

A safe DSCR portfolio staggers loan maturities, mixes fixed and adjustable loans, and avoids excessive reliance on interest-only structures. It also keeps enough margin so that even if rates rise, the portfolio can survive without forced sales.

Understanding loan structure is just as important as choosing the right property. DSCR risk is not only about cash flow. It is about timing, resets, and how your loans behave under pressure.

How Interest Rate Risk Can Break or Protect a DSCR Portfolio

Assume an investor owns four DSCR properties. Each rents for $3,200 per month. Each has a loan of $400,000 at 7 percent interest-only. The monthly payment is about $2,333. Taxes, insurance, and maintenance total $700. That makes total expenses $3,033. Each property cash flows $167.

Across four properties, the portfolio produces $668 per month. It looks stable.

Now assume the interest-only period ends and the loans convert to principal and interest at 9 percent. The new payment becomes about $3,200. Total expenses become

$3,900. With rent still at $3,200, each property loses $700. Across four properties, the investor now loses $2,800 per month.

If the investor planned for this, they would have reserves. If not, they are in trouble.

Now imagine instead the investor chose 30-year fixed DSCR loans at 7.5 percent. The payment is about $2,800. Total expenses become $3,500. Cash flow is negative $300 per property. But the payment never changes. When rents rise to $3,600 in two years, the property becomes profitable.

The first investor was profitable first but fragile later. The second was tight early but safe long-term. That is how loan structure controls risk.

DSCR risk is not about what works today. It is about what survives tomorrow.

Chapter 4

Vacancy, Tenant Risk, and Income Stability

Vacancy is the most underestimated risk in DSCR investing because it does not appear in the underwriting formula. DSCR is calculated using gross rental income divided by the mortgage payment, which assumes full occupancy and perfect collections. Real life does not operate that way. Tenants move. Units require repairs. Markets cool. Tourism slows. Employers leave cities. None of these risks are accounted for in the DSCR ratio, yet they are the primary drivers of real-world failure. Investors who do not build their portfolios around vacancy management are not actually managing risk; they are ignoring it and hoping it does not appear.

DSCR portfolios are uniquely sensitive to vacancy because they are built on leverage. When a property is purchased with 70 to 80 percent debt, the rent must perform continuously to support that debt. A single vacant month means the mortgage must be paid from reserves or other properties. When multiple vacancies occur at the same time, the portfolio can rapidly go from profitable to distressed. This is why professional investors never evaluate vacancy as a temporary inconvenience. They treat it as a structural cost that must be planned for in advance.

Tenant risk is not just about whether someone pays rent. It includes how long they stay, how much damage they cause, how often they turn over, and how likely they are to create legal or maintenance issues. High-turnover tenants increase vacancy, increase repair costs, and reduce net operating income. Short-term tenants produce higher gross rents but higher volatility. Long-term tenants produce lower gross rents but more stability. DSCR portfolios must balance these forces. A portfolio built entirely on high-volatility tenants is extremely fragile, even if DSCR looks strong on paper.

Income stability is more important than maximum income. Many investors chase the highest possible rent without realizing that volatility is a hidden tax. A property that earns $3,200 every month is safer than a property that earns $4,000 some months and $1,500 in others. DSCR underwriting averages income, but risk management must evaluate the worst-case months. If your mortgage is due every month, your income must be reliable every month. That is why DSCR investors should always model their cash flow using conservative rent assumptions rather than peak rents.

Another major factor in vacancy risk is geographic and market concentration. A portfolio of ten rentals in one city is far more dangerous than a portfolio of ten rentals across three cities. If that city suffers job losses, insurance spikes, or regulatory changes, the entire portfolio is affected at once. Professional DSCR investors spread properties across multiple markets, tenant types, and rental models so that income streams are not perfectly correlated. Correlation is what turns small problems into portfolio-wide crises.

Lease structure also plays a critical role in income stability. Month-to-month leases increase flexibility but also increase turnover. Annual leases create stability but reduce flexibility. Mid-term leases serve traveling professionals but fluctuate seasonally. Short-term rentals fluctuate weekly. Each model has a place, but stacking only one type magnifies risk. A balanced DSCR portfolio includes multiple lease lengths so that not all tenants can leave at once.

Property condition is another hidden vacancy risk. Poorly maintained properties attract poor tenants and create longer vacancies when they turn. High-quality units rent faster, hold tenants longer, and require fewer costly turnovers. Maintenance spending is not an expense. It is vacancy prevention. Investors who cut maintenance to maximize cash flow often create longer and more expensive vacancies later.

The final layer of vacancy risk is reserve planning. Even the best tenant profile will eventually fail. Tenants lose jobs, relocate, or experience life events. Risk management does not try to prevent vacancies. It makes vacancies survivable. A DSCR portfolio should have enough reserves to carry all properties through multiple months of zero rent. Without reserves, the investor is one eviction away from distress.

Vacancy does not destroy portfolios instantly. It erodes them. First comes a missed payment. Then a credit card is used. Then another property covers the loss. Then reserves are gone. Then refinancing becomes impossible. Then forced selling begins. All of this starts with unplanned vacancy. Investors who control vacancy control the destiny of their DSCR portfolios.

How Vacancy Turns a Profitable DSCR Portfolio Into a Financial Crisis

Assume an investor owns eight DSCR rental properties. Each rents for $2,900 per month. Each mortgage payment is $2,200. Taxes, insurance, maintenance, and management average $500 per property. That makes the total monthly cost $2,700. Each property produces $200 of true cash flow. Across eight properties, that is $1,600 per month. On paper, the portfolio looks healthy.

Now assume two tenants leave at the same time. Those two properties produce zero income but still cost $2,700 each. That is $5,400 in negative cash flow. The remaining six properties produce $1,200. That means the portfolio now loses $4,200 per month. If the vacancies last three months, the investor needs $12,600 just to keep loans current.

Now assume one vacant property also needs $6,000 in repairs before it can be rented again. The total required cash becomes $18,600. If the investor had been saving the $1,600 per month for reserves, after twelve months they would have $19,200. They survive. If they had spent it on new purchases, they fail.

Now imagine a diversified portfolio. Four properties are long-term rentals at $2,600. Four are mid-term rentals at $3,200. The average rent is still $2,900. Two long-term tenants leave. The lost income is $5,200 instead of $5,800. The mid-term units still perform. The monthly loss is $3,600 instead of $4,200. The portfolio bleeds slower and survives longer.

This is how DSCR risk management works. It is not about avoiding vacancies. It is about structuring income, reserves, and tenant types so that vacancies do not control your future.

Chapter 5

Leverage Stacking, Cross-Collateralization, and Domino Risk

One of the most powerful features of DSCR lending is that it allows investors to repeatedly use leverage to grow a rental portfolio far faster than conventional financing would allow. The danger is that this same power can quietly turn into a chain of financial dependencies where one weak property can destabilize every other asset you own. This is called leverage stacking, and it is the primary way DSCR portfolios collapse during economic stress. Investors do not fail because one property goes bad. They fail because multiple properties are financially tied together without sufficient separation.

Leverage stacking occurs when the cash flow or equity from one property is used to support another property, which is then used to support another. It often happens through HELOCs, cash-out refinances, blanket loans, portfolio loans, or business credit lines secured by real estate. Each layer of leverage looks reasonable by itself, but together they create a structure where no single property is truly independent. When one asset suffers, it pulls on the others like dominoes.

Cross-collateralization is the most dangerous form of leverage stacking. This occurs when multiple properties are pledged as collateral for one loan. The lender now has the legal right to seize all of them if one part of the loan fails. Investors often use cross-collateralization to get better terms or to access more capital, but they rarely understand how much risk they are adding. A single vacancy, repair, or rent drop on one property can now put multiple properties at risk.

Even without formal cross-collateralization, investors often create informal cross-collateralization by using cash flow from one property to cover shortfalls on another. This is how portfolios slowly bleed to death. The strong properties are forced to subsidize the weak ones until nothing is left. Professional investors isolate risk so that each property stands on its own financially.

The safest DSCR portfolios are built so that every property can survive independently. That means each property must have enough margin and reserves to cover its own problems without pulling money from others. Portfolio-level reserves exist to cover systemic shocks, not to bail out permanently weak deals.

Another hidden danger is stacking adjustable loans. If several DSCR loans reset in the same year, a single rate spike can raise payments across the entire portfolio simultaneously. This is not diversification. It is synchronized risk. Smart investors stagger loan maturities so that not all risk arrives at once. Leverage is not bad. It is what creates wealth. But leverage must be compartmentalized. Each loan should be a tool, not a trap. Risk management means designing your debt so that problems stay local instead of spreading.

How Leverage Stacking Creates Domino Risk

An investor owns three rental properties. Each rents for $3,000. Each has a DSCR loan of $2,100 and expenses of $500. Each produces $400 per month. The total portfolio cash flow is $1,200.

The investor uses a HELOC secured on Property A to buy Property D. Property D produces only $100 per month. Now Property A must cover the HELOC payment of $300. Property A's cash flow drops from $400 to $100.

Now Property A and D are financially tied. If either suffers, both are at risk.

Then a tenant leaves Property D. Property D loses $3,000 per month. Property A must now cover both its own expenses and Property D's mortgage and HELOC. Property A goes negative. Soon all properties are being drained.

If instead the investor had used reserves or waited for stronger cash flow, the problem would be contained.

This is why professional DSCR investors never let one property's survival depend on another.

Chapter 6

Stress Testing Your DSCR Portfolio Before the Market Does

The most dangerous thing an investor can believe is that today's cash flow will always exist tomorrow. DSCR loans are approved based on current rents, current rates, and current expenses, but markets are never static. Rents fluctuate, insurance rises, property taxes change, and interest rates move in cycles. Stress testing is the process of intentionally breaking your own portfolio on paper before the market tries to break it in real life. Investors who do not stress test are not risk managing. They are guessing.

Stress testing means modeling how your portfolio performs under negative conditions. You assume vacancies. You assume rent drops. You assume expense increases. You assume rate resets. Then you calculate how long your portfolio survives before it becomes insolvent. This is how professional landlords and real estate funds evaluate investments. They never ask, "How much will this make if everything goes right?" They ask, "How much can this lose before it fails?"

DSCR portfolios must be stress tested at both the property level and the portfolio level. A property might survive a 10 percent rent drop, but what happens when four properties experience it at the same time? A loan might be safe at today's rate, but what happens when it resets three percent higher? Stress testing forces you to confront the real limits of your leverage.

The first variable in stress testing is income. You reduce rents by five percent, ten percent, or more and see what happens to DSCR and cash flow. The second variable is vacancy. You model one month, three months, or six months of no rent. The third variable is expenses. You increase insurance, taxes, and maintenance. The fourth variable is debt. You raise interest rates or add principal payments.

Stress testing shows you whether your portfolio bends or breaks. A resilient portfolio loses money but survives. A fragile portfolio defaults.

Stress testing is not pessimism. It is preparation. When you know your break points, you can set reserves, loan structures, and growth speed accordingly.

Stress Testing a Five-Property DSCR Portfolio

An investor owns five rentals. Each rents for $3,200. Each mortgage is $2,300. Expenses are $600. Total cost is $2,900. Cash flow is $300 per property, or $1,500 total. Now stress test one: rents drop 10 percent to $2,880. Costs stay $2,900. Each property loses $20. The portfolio loses $100 per month. With $60,000 in reserves, the portfolio survives 600 months.

Stress test two: two vacancies. Income drops by $6,400. Remaining income is $9,600. Costs remain $14,500. Loss is $4,900. With $60,000, survival is 12 months.

Stress test three: rates rise $400. Mortgages become $2,700. Total cost becomes $3,300. With rent at $3,200, loss is $100 per property, or $500 total.

This math tells the investor how much risk they really have.

This is how professionals protect DSCR portfolios.

Chapter 7

Liquidity, Exit Options, and Never Being Forced to Sell

The single most important advantage a DSCR investor can have is not high cash flow or fast growth, but liquidity. Liquidity is the ability to survive without selling. Every real estate disaster begins the same way. The investor runs out of cash. Once cash is gone, choices disappear. When choices disappear, properties are sold at the worst possible time. DSCR portfolios that collapse do not fail because the real estate was bad. They fail because the investor lost the ability to wait.

Liquidity turns risk into opportunity. When markets fall, rents soften, or interest rates rise, investors with liquidity can hold, refinance, or buy. Investors without liquidity are forced to sell. DSCR leverage amplifies this effect. Because DSCR loans are based on property income rather than personal income, the portfolio itself must be liquid enough to survive downturns. When liquidity is weak, leverage becomes a weapon against the investor.

Exit options are the second pillar of survival. Every property must have more than one way out. It must be able to sell, refinance, or be converted to a different rental strategy. A property that only works under one scenario is a trap. A property that works under three scenarios is an asset. Risk management is about building exits into every deal before you buy it.

Liquidity is created through reserves, credit lines, equity, and diversification. Reserves allow you to pay when income stops. Credit lines allow you to bridge gaps. Equity allows you to refinance or sell without loss. Diversification ensures not all income stops at once. Together, these create financial gravity that keeps you anchored when markets shift.

The worst DSCR portfolios are those that are profitable but illiquid. They produce cash flow but have no reserves, no credit lines, and no exit flexibility. When stress arrives, they implode. The best portfolios may grow slower, but they are unstoppable.

Professional investors always ask one question: How long can I survive if nothing works? If the answer is six months, the portfolio is fragile. If the answer is two years, the portfolio is powerful. Time is the ultimate risk buffer.

How Liquidity Prevents Forced Sales

An investor owns six DSCR rentals producing $1,200 per month. They have $10,000 in cash. A recession hits. Two tenants leave. Monthly loss becomes $4,000. In 2.5 months, cash is gone. They must sell.

Another investor owns the same portfolio but has $100,000 in reserves and a $50,000 HELOC. They can survive 37 months of losses. During that time, rents recover. They refinance. They survive.

The difference is liquidity. Not property quality. Not DSCR. Liquidity.

Chapter 8

Diversification, Market Cycles, and Portfolio Resilience

Most DSCR investors believe diversification simply means owning more properties. In reality, diversification means owning properties that do not fail at the same time. A portfolio of ten rentals in the same zip code is not diversified. It is concentrated risk. When a market slows, rents fall, insurance rises, or regulations change, every property is hit at once. DSCR leverage amplifies this effect because debt remains fixed even when income does not. True risk management requires diversification across geography, tenant type, rental model, and economic drivers.

Market cycles are unavoidable. Every city experiences booms and contractions. Employment grows and contracts. Housing supply rises and falls. Tourism surges and drops. When DSCR investors ignore cycles, they end up buying at peaks and financing at the worst times. When they respect cycles, they buy across multiple phases and protect cash flow.

Geographic diversification is the first defense. A property in Orlando behaves differently from one in Ohio or Texas. Insurance risks, job markets, rent growth, and regulatory environments are not the same. A DSCR portfolio spread across multiple states does not move in lockstep. This reduces volatility and protects income.

Tenant diversification is the second layer. Long-term renters, short-term guests, traveling nurses, students, retirees, and families all respond differently to economic shifts. A portfolio that includes multiple tenant profiles will always have income flowing from somewhere.

Rental model diversification is equally important. Short-term rentals perform well in booms but drop in recessions. Long-term rentals are stable but grow slower. Mid-term rentals bridge the two. A balanced DSCR portfolio includes all three.

Diversification creates resilience. Resilience is what allows leverage to work safely. Without it, DSCR becomes a ticking clock.

How Diversification Protects DSCR Income

Investor A owns eight short-term rentals in one city. Each averages $3,500 in high season but drops to $1,800 in low season. Mortgages and expenses are $2,500. In slow season, each loses $700. Across eight units, that is $5,600 per month in losses. Investor B owns four long-term rentals at $2,600 and four mid-term rentals at $3,200. Mortgages and expenses are also $2,500. The long-term units make $100. The mid-term make $700. Even if two mid-term units go vacant, the long-term units stabilize the portfolio.

Diversification keeps cash flow alive when cycles turn.

Chapter 9

Monitoring, Early Warning Signals, and Portfolio Corrections

The greatest risk in a DSCR portfolio is not a sudden crash. It is slow decay that goes unnoticed until it becomes irreversible. Most investors only react when they miss a payment or when a lender sends a warning letter. Professional DSCR investors monitor their portfolios the way pilots monitor aircraft systems. They look for early warning signs that tell them something is changing long before a crisis appears. Risk management is not a one-time event at purchase. It is an ongoing system of measurement, review, and correction.

Every DSCR portfolio has financial vital signs just like a human body. These include rent trends, vacancy rates, operating expense ratios, DSCR ratios, reserve levels, and loan-to-value. When any of these begin to move in the wrong direction, it signals growing risk. A slight drop in rent may not seem dangerous, but if it is combined with rising insurance and increasing vacancy, it creates a compounding effect that weakens the entire portfolio. Investors who only look at their bank balance miss these deeper signals. DSCR itself should be monitored monthly, not just at refinance time. If your portfolio DSCR is falling, it means your margin of safety is shrinking. A portfolio that once had a DSCR of 1.35 may drift down to 1.15 over time as expenses rise. That change may seem small, but it dramatically reduces your ability to refinance, absorb rate increases, or handle vacancies. Once DSCR falls below lender minimums, options disappear.

Vacancy trends are another powerful signal. If it takes longer to fill units, something in the market has changed. This may be increased supply, reduced demand, or declining tenant quality. Longer vacancy means higher burn rate. Monitoring days-on-market and tenant turnover allows you to react early by adjusting pricing, improving property condition, or changing rental strategy.

Expense creep is one of the most dangerous risks because it happens quietly. Insurance renewals, property taxes, utilities, HOA fees, and maintenance all tend to rise over time. When these costs increase faster than rents, your DSCR declines even if properties are fully occupied. Professional investors track operating expense ratios so they can identify when a property is becoming inefficient.

Loan metrics also provide early warnings. Rising loan-to-value means you are losing equity. Adjustable-rate reset dates approaching mean payment risk is increasing. Balloon payments approaching mean refinance risk is growing.

Ignoring loan timelines is how investors get trapped.

The purpose of monitoring is not to panic. It is to correct. When early signals appear, you can raise rents, refinance, sell underperforming assets, restructure debt, or add reserves. Waiting until a crisis means you no longer have these options.

DSCR risk management is dynamic. It requires dashboards, monthly reviews, and honest assessment. The investor who measures stays in control. The investor who guesses eventually loses control.

How Early Warning Signals Save a DSCR Portfolio

An investor owns seven DSCR rentals. Each rents for $3,000. Each mortgage is $2,200. Expenses are $600. Total cost is $2,800. Cash flow is $200 per property, or $1,400 total.

In year one, insurance rises by $100 per unit. New cost is $2,900. Cash flow drops to $100 per property, or $700 total. DSCR also falls.

In year two, property taxes increase by $50 per unit. Costs become $2,950. Cash flow is now $50 per property, or $350 total.

Vacancy rises slightly. One unit goes empty for one month. Loss is $2,950. That wipes out eight months of profit.

If the investor was monitoring, they would have raised rents or sold a weak property before this happened. Instead, reserves are now shrinking.

Now imagine the investor saw this trend early. They raised rents $150 across the portfolio. New rent is $3,150. Costs are $2,950. Cash flow becomes $200 per property again. DSCR stabilizes. The portfolio survives.

Monitoring turns small problems into manageable adjustments instead of disasters.

Chapter 10

Long-Term Risk, Exit Timing, and Portfolio Sustainability

Most investors think of real estate in terms of purchases, not exits. Yet every DSCR loan you take out is a temporary structure that must eventually be refinanced, paid off, or sold. Long-term risk is not about what happens this year. It is about whether your portfolio can still exist ten, twenty, or thirty years from now. DSCR lending gives investors incredible speed and scale, but it also compresses timelines. Loans reset. Balloons come due. Markets cycle. Sustainability is the ability to survive all of them without losing control.

Exit planning must be done before you buy. A property should never be purchased based on one outcome. It should have multiple profitable exits. It should be rentable long term, sellable to retail buyers, refinancable under conventional or DSCR terms, and convertible to another rental strategy. A property that only works under one scenario is a liability, not an asset.

Time is the hidden risk. The longer you hold a leveraged asset, the more chances there are for rates, taxes, insurance, and regulations to change. A sustainable DSCR portfolio assumes that conditions will worsen at some point and plans for it financially.

Equity is your ultimate safety net. High leverage is powerful early, but over time, paying down principal and growing value creates options. Equity allows you to refinance, sell without loss, or pivot strategies. Investors who only chase cash flow and ignore equity are building fragile portfolios.

Sustainable DSCR investing is about transitioning from high leverage to low leverage over time. Early in the portfolio, you use DSCR to grow. Later, you use equity to stabilize. This is how institutional landlords operate. They use debt to acquire, then they let time and rent growth de-risk the portfolio.

Exit timing is not about guessing the top. It is about reading your own risk metrics. When DSCR declines, reserves shrink, and loan resets approach, risk is rising. That is when you sell or refinance. When DSCR is strong, equity is high, and liquidity is deep, you hold or buy.

This chapter teaches you how to think decades ahead instead of deal by deal. That is how DSCR wealth becomes permanent.

How Exit Planning Prevents Portfolio Collapse

An investor buys five DSCR properties at 75 percent LTV. Each is worth $400,000. Each loan is $300,000. After five years, rents rise and values grow to $500,000. Loans are still $290,000. Equity per property is now $210,000.

The investor refinances two properties, pulling out $200,000 total while still maintaining safe DSCR. They use it to pay down two other loans. Now the portfolio is safer.

If the market turns, they have options. If they had stayed fully leveraged, they would be trapped.

This is how long-term DSCR wealth is protected.

Chapter 11

Building a DSCR Portfolio That Survives Any Economy

A DSCR portfolio that only works when the economy is strong is not a real investment system. It is a fair-weather machine that collapses when conditions change. True wealth is built by portfolios that can survive recessions, inflation, rising interest rates, job losses, housing oversupply, and government policy shifts. The goal of DSCR risk management is not to avoid downturns. It is to design your portfolio so that downturns become periods of consolidation rather than destruction.

The first principle of an all-weather DSCR portfolio is margin. Margin is the space between what your properties earn and what they must pay. When margin is thin, small shocks become large problems. When margin is thick, even large shocks are survivable. Professional investors always sacrifice some short-term growth to protect long-term margin. They would rather own five safe properties than ten fragile ones.

The second principle is liquidity. Liquidity is time. Time allows rents to recover. Time allows refinances. Time allows markets to heal. DSCR portfolios without liquidity are always racing against the clock. The moment cash runs out, options disappear. Liquidity is what transforms leverage from a threat into a tool.

The third principle is structural resilience. This means no single property, tenant, market, or loan can destroy the whole portfolio. Each asset must stand on its own. Each loan must be survivable on its own. Each market must be able to fail without taking everything with it. This is how institutions build portfolios that last generations.

The fourth principle is flexibility. A resilient DSCR portfolio can change strategies when conditions change. A long-term rental can become a mid-term rental. A short-term rental can become a long-term rental. A property can be sold, refinanced, or repurposed. Flexibility prevents you from being trapped.

The fifth principle is continuous measurement. You must always know your DSCR, your reserves, your vacancy rate, and your debt exposure. Investors who stop measuring slowly drift into danger.

An all-weather DSCR portfolio is not built by chasing returns. It is built by controlling risk. When risk is controlled, returns compound for decades.

How an All-Weather DSCR Portfolio Survives a Recession

An investor owns ten DSCR rentals. Each rents for $3,000.

Each mortgage is $2,100. Expenses are $600. Each property produces $300 per month, or $3,000 total.

The investor holds $120,000 in reserves. That covers 40 months of full expenses for one property or 10 months for all ten.

A recession hits. Rents fall 10 percent to $2,700. Costs remain $2,700. Cash flow drops to zero. Two properties go vacant. Monthly loss becomes $5,400.

With $120,000 in reserves, the investor can survive 22 months of losses. During that time, rents recover. Vacancies fill. The portfolio survives.

A leveraged investor without reserves would be wiped out.

This is what separates permanent DSCR wealth from temporary success.

Chapter 12

Turning Risk Into Strategic Advantage

Risk is not the enemy of DSCR investors. Unmanaged risk is. When risk is measured, structured, and planned for, it becomes the engine that creates outsized wealth. The purpose of every risk management system in this book is not to make you conservative. It is to make you unstoppable. Investors who understand their downside always outperform investors who only focus on upside, because they can move aggressively without being fragile.

DSCR loans are designed for professional investors. Banks expect you to manage cash flow, reserves, and portfolio structure like a business, not like a homeowner. When you do, DSCR financing allows you to buy more, scale faster, and deploy capital more efficiently than almost any other real estate strategy in existence. The key is that every dollar of leverage must be paired with a dollar of control.

Strategic risk means using leverage when the odds are in your favor and pulling back when they are not. It means adding properties when DSCR margins are high and liquidity is deep. It means slowing purchases when expenses rise, vacancies increase, or interest rates reset. Professional investors do not grow constantly. They grow in cycles.

One of the most powerful risk tools is selective selling. Selling a weak property during a strong market can make the rest of the portfolio dramatically safer. Reducing one loan can increase DSCR, improve liquidity, and lower portfolio-wide risk more than buying another property ever could.

Refinancing is another strategic weapon. When rates fall or rents rise, DSCR improves. That allows you to pull equity or lock in better terms. Investors who track their metrics know exactly when to refinance.

The final level of strategic risk is capital redeployment. When one market becomes overheated or unstable, capital is moved to safer or higher-growth markets. DSCR investors who operate this way are not landlords. They are capital managers.

This is how risk becomes power.

How Strategic Risk Creates DSCR Wealth

An investor owns eight DSCR properties worth $500,000 each. Loans are $350,000 each. Equity is $150,000 per property, or $1.2 million total. Rents rise and DSCR improves. The investor refinances two properties, pulling $200,000. They use that to pay off one loan. Now one property is debt-free.

That one property produces $3,000 per month. It now stabilizes the entire portfolio.

If a recession hits, they have a safety anchor. That is how strategic risk turns leverage into permanent wealth.

Chapter 13

The Risk-Adjusted DSCR Investor Playbook

The final evolution of a DSCR investor is not the one who owns the most properties, but the one who controls the most outcomes. Risk-adjusted investing means you do not ask how much you can borrow, but how much you can safely control across multiple market cycles. This chapter brings together every risk concept in this book into a single operational framework that allows you to scale aggressively while remaining nearly impossible to destroy financially.

Every DSCR portfolio exists inside a triangle of constraints: cash flow, liquidity, and debt structure. Cash flow determines how much income your assets produce. Liquidity determines how long you can survive when income fails. Debt structure determines how flexible or fragile your obligations are. When any one of these becomes weak, the entire portfolio becomes unstable. Risk-adjusted investors continuously rebalance these three elements.

The playbook begins with margin first. Every property must produce not just DSCR-qualified income, but true economic surplus after all real expenses. Professional DSCR investors target at least 15 to 25 percent margin above total costs. That margin feeds reserves, funds growth, and absorbs shocks. Properties that only barely meet DSCR are not growth assets. They are risk amplifiers.

The second layer is reserve velocity. Reserves are not a static pile of money. They must grow in proportion to portfolio size. As more DSCR loans are added, required reserves rise. A portfolio with ten properties needs far more protection than a portfolio with two. Risk-adjusted investors set reserve targets based on months of total portfolio burn rate, not on feelings.

The third layer is debt timing. Loans must be staggered. Adjustable-rate resets, balloon payments, and refinance windows should never cluster in the same year. If they do, the portfolio becomes exposed to rate cycles. A safe DSCR investor spreads maturities so that even the worst interest-rate environment only affects part of the portfolio at a time.

The fourth layer is asset hierarchy. Every DSCR portfolio must contain "anchor properties." These are lower-leverage, higher-cash-flow assets that stabilize everything else. Not every property should be maximally leveraged. Some should exist purely to generate safety and liquidity.

The fifth layer is dynamic correction. You do not wait for distress. When DSCR trends down, reserves thin, or vacancies rise, you take action. You raise rents, refinance, sell weak properties, or slow acquisitions. This keeps the system balanced.

Risk-adjusted DSCR investing is not about being cautious. It is about being precise. When every part of the system is monitored and structured, you can scale faster than anyone else because you are not afraid of volatility.

Building a Risk-Adjusted DSCR Portfolio That Cannot Collapse

An investor begins with three DSCR rental properties. Each property is purchased for $400,000 with a 75 percent DSCR loan of $300,000. Each rents for $3,200 per month. Each mortgage payment is $2,200. Taxes, insurance, and maintenance average $600. That makes total costs $2,800. Cash flow is $400 per property, or $1,200 total. Instead of spending this $1,200, the investor puts it into reserves. After one year, reserves are $14,400.

In year two, the investor buys two more properties with the same numbers. Now there are five properties producing $2,000 per month in total cash flow. The investor continues saving. At the end of year two, reserves are $38,400. In year three, one tenant leaves and one roof costs $10,000. Instead of panic, the investor pays it from reserves. Rents are raised by

$150 across all units. New rent is $3,350. New cash flow becomes $550 per property, or $2,750 total.

In year four, interest rates rise and one loan resets, increasing the mortgage by $300. That property's cash flow drops from $550 to $250. But because the portfolio includes four other strong properties, the portfolio remains profitable. No distress occurs.

By year five, the investor has $90,000 in reserves. They sell one weak property for $450,000 and pay off its $290,000 loan. That produces $160,000. They use $120,000 to pay down two other loans. Now two properties have far lower payments and high cash flow.

The portfolio now produces more income, has lower risk, and is more stable than ever. This is what risk-adjusted DSCR investing looks like.

Chapter 14

Crisis Management, Recovery, and Portfolio Rebuilding

No DSCR investor, no matter how skilled, will avoid stress forever. Markets cycle, tenants fail, interest rates reset, and unexpected events occur. The difference between investors who become wealthy and those who are wiped out is not whether they experience crises, but how they respond to them. Crisis management is not panic. It is a system. This chapter gives you that system.

The first phase of crisis is recognition. Problems rarely appear overnight. They show up as rising vacancy, declining DSCR, shrinking reserves, or increasing expenses. Investors who track their numbers see danger early. Investors who do not only see it when payments are missed. Early recognition allows for soft corrections instead of emergency decisions.

The second phase is liquidity defense. When income drops, the only thing that matters is cash. Liquidity buys time. Time allows you to negotiate, refinance, raise rents, re-tenant, or sell strategically. The moment liquidity runs out, every option becomes bad. Professional DSCR investors protect liquidity before they protect growth. The third phase is triage. Not all properties are equal. Some should be saved. Some should be sold. Some should be restructured. Triage means ranking assets by their risk and contribution to portfolio stability. Weak assets are removed first to protect strong ones.

The fourth phase is stabilization. Once the bleeding stops, the goal is to rebuild margin, rebuild reserves, and reduce leverage. This is done through rent increases, expense control, refinancing, and selective paydowns.

The final phase is growth reset. After stability is restored, acquisitions can resume — but only under safer, stronger criteria than before. Every crisis is a chance to upgrade the portfolio.

This is how DSCR investors survive storms and emerge stronger than before.

How a DSCR Investor Survives a Market Crash and Comes Back Stronger

An investor owns ten DSCR rentals. Each rents for $3,100. Each mortgage is $2,300. Expenses average $600. Total cost is $2,900. Cash flow is $200 per property, or $2,000 per month. The investor has $80,000 in reserves. A recession hits. Three tenants leave. Income drops by $9,300. Remaining income is $21,700. Costs remain $29,000. Monthly loss is $7,300. In 11 months, reserves would be gone.

The investor immediately sells two weak properties for $420,000 each. Loans are $300,000 each. Net cash is $240,000. They use $120,000 to pay off two loans. Now two properties are debt-free. Those two produce $6,200 in rent.

The portfolio is now eight properties with lower debt and higher stability. Losses drop to $1,500 per month. Reserves recover. Within a year rents rebound. The investor survives and now owns safer assets.

This is how crisis becomes opportunity.

Final Thoughts

Real estate has always rewarded those who understand risk more than those who chase returns. DSCR lending did not change this truth. It simply magnified it. When investors can borrow based on rental income instead of personal income, the scale of opportunity expands, but so does the scale of responsibility. This book was written to close the gap between what most investors are taught and what professional portfolio builders actually do. DSCR loans are not dangerous. Unstructured leverage is.

The greatest illusion in modern real estate investing is that more properties equal more safety. In reality, safety comes from margin, liquidity, diversification, and control. A portfolio with ten thinly margined properties is far more fragile than a portfolio with five well-capitalized, properly structured assets. The difference is not intelligence or ambition. It is design. Throughout this book, you have learned that DSCR success is not about deal volume. It is about system integrity.

The investors who last decades in this business do not avoid downturns. They survive them. They understand that rent cycles change, interest rates move, and expenses rise. They plan for it. They do not panic. They reposition. They do not liquidate in fear. They redeploy with precision. That is what separates wealth builders from deal chasers.

You now understand that risk in DSCR investing is not a mystery. It is measurable. Vacancy, interest rates, expenses, leverage stacking, loan resets, liquidity, and exit options are not random forces. They are variables that can be modeled, monitored, and controlled. When you take the time to structure your portfolio properly, you become resilient to forces that destroy less prepared investors.

DSCR financing gives you the ability to operate like a professional landlord, even as an individual investor. You can separate your personal income from your investment activity. You can scale faster. You can keep more of your money working. But that only works when you operate like a business, not a hobbyist. That means you track DSCR, reserves, loan maturities, and portfolio health with the same discipline that banks use when they lend you money.

The greatest gift of DSCR lending is optionality. When you have margin, liquidity, and strong structure, you get to choose when to sell, refinance, or buy. When you do not, the market chooses for you. Everything in this book is designed to keep you in control of that choice. If you apply what you have learned here, you will not fear market cycles. You will use them. You will buy when others cannot. You will hold when others are forced to sell. And over time, you will build something that does not just survive — it compounds.

This is not how most people invest. That is why most people never build lasting real estate wealth. You now have the framework that institutions use. The only question left is whether you will use it.

The Professional Guide to DSCR, Rental Loans & Passive Income Financing: Series Roadmap

This series was created to give real estate investors a complete, professional-grade financing system for building long-term rental wealth. Each book builds on the last, guiding readers from their first DSCR loan through the creation of a fully optimized rental portfolio and passive income machine.

Whether you are buying your first rental or managing a multi-property empire, this roadmap shows you exactly where you are and where to go next.

Book 1 – DSCR Loan Fundamentals

How Debt Service Coverage Ratio Loans Really Work

This foundational volume explains the mechanics of DSCR loans. You learn how lenders calculate income, payments, risk, and approval decisions. This book gives you the mathematical and strategic framework needed to evaluate any rental property and determine whether it qualifies for DSCR financing.

Book 2 – How to Qualify for a DSCR Loan

The Step-by-Step Investor Approval Playbook

This book takes you inside the DSCR approval process. You will learn how to prepare your credit, structure your finances, choose the right entity, and submit loan files that get approved faster and with better terms.

Book 3 – DSCR vs Conventional & Hard Money

How Smart Investors Choose the Right Financing

This volume shows how DSCR loans compare to traditional mortgages and hard money. You will learn when to use each type of financing and how to combine them for maximum growth and minimum risk.

Book 4 – DSCR Loans for Short-Term Rentals

How Airbnb & VRBO Investors Get Approved

Learn how DSCR lenders evaluate short-term rental income, how Airbnb projections are used, and how to structure vacation rental deals that qualify for investor financing.

Book 5 – DSCR Loans for Multi-Family & Portfolios

How to Finance Duplexes, Triplexes, and 10+ Property Portfolios

This book shows how DSCR loans are used to finance multi-unit properties and entire rental portfolios, including how lenders analyze large groups of properties and how investors scale beyond single-family homes.

Book 6 – No-Income DSCR Loans

How to Get Approved Without Tax Returns or Paystubs

This volume explains how investors with low or zero taxable income use DSCR loans to continue buying property, even when traditional banks would say no.

Book 7 – Using DSCR Loans to Scale Faster

How Investors Buy More Properties Without Hitting DTI Limits

Learn how DSCR loans remove personal income ceilings and allow investors to build large portfolios using property cash flow instead of W-2 income.

Book 8 – DSCR Loans for Foreign Nationals & LLCs

How International and Business Buyers Finance U.S. Property

This book covers how DSCR loans work for LLCs, partnerships, foreign buyers, and entity-based real estate strategies.

Book 9 – DSCR Risk Management

How to Use Leverage Without Blowing Up Your Portfolio

You will learn how to stress-test deals, manage leverage, and protect your portfolio from market downturns, vacancies, and rising expenses.

Book 10 – The Investor Financing Blueprint

How to Build a Rental Empire Using DSCR Loans

This final book ties everything together into a complete long-term system for building passive income, financial independence, and generational wealth through DSCR-powered real estate.

About the Author

Joseph G. Correa is a licensed mortgage broker, real estate finance strategist, and the founder of **Finibi Mortgage**, where he specializes in investor financing, DSCR loans, rental portfolio funding, and alternative real estate lending solutions. With years of experience structuring residential and business-purpose mortgage programs, Joseph has helped real estate investors, entrepreneurs, and business owners access millions of dollars in capital to acquire, refinance, and scale income-producing property.

Unlike traditional lenders who focus on W-2 income and rigid debt-to-income formulas, Joseph's work centers on **asset-based and cash-flow-driven financing**, allowing investors to qualify based on property performance instead of personal tax returns. His expertise spans DSCR loans, no-income investor mortgages, LLC and portfolio financing, short-term rental lending, and advanced leverage strategies used by professional real estate operators.

Through **Finibi Mortgage**, Joseph works with a wide network of national lenders to deliver flexible investor loan programs for single-family rentals, multi-family properties, Airbnb and vacation rentals, and large rental portfolios. His clients include first-time rental buyers, seasoned landlords, real estate syndicators, foreign national investors, and business owners who want to build passive income without being limited by conventional banking rules.

Joseph is also the publisher of the **Investor Mortgage Wealth Series**, a professional education platform designed to give investors a clear, transparent understanding of how real estate financing really works. This series was created to eliminate confusion, expose hidden lending rules, and empower readers to make confident, profitable financing decisions.

His mission is simple: **to give investors access to the same financing strategies used by institutional real estate buyers so they can build long-term wealth, freedom, and financial security through property ownership.**

How to Get a Personalized Investor DSCR Review

If you found this book helpful, you may want to see how these DSCR strategies apply to your specific investment property, rental income, and financing goals.

Every real estate investor's situation is different. Loan programs, interest rates, DSCR requirements, and available options vary based on property type, rental income, credit profile, entity structure, and state guidelines. The examples in this book are educational, but your personal DSCR eligibility and pricing can only be determined through an individualized review.

As a licensed mortgage broker, I offer a **Personalized Investor DSCR Review** designed to show you:

• Whether your current or target property qualifies for DSCR financing• How much you can borrow based on real rental income• What down payment and interest rate ranges apply to your situation• How to structure the loan for the strongest DSCR and cash flow• How to finance through an LLC, partnership, or personal name• Which DSCR programs are best for your goals

This review is fast, confidential, and focused entirely on helping you make better investment decisions.

To request your personalized DSCR review, visit:

https://investordscr.carrd.co/

There you can submit your property details and receive a professional assessment of your DSCR financing options or through this QR code:

Your property already has a story.This review shows you how lenders will read it.

Yours truly,

Joseph G. Correa

Educational & Financial Disclaimer

This publication is provided for educational and informational purposes only. The author and publisher are not engaged in rendering legal, financial, accounting, investment, tax, or mortgage advice. The content of this book is intended to provide general information about real estate investing, Debt Service Coverage Ratio (DSCR) loans, and mortgage financing strategies, but it does not constitute professional advice.

All examples, calculations, and scenarios presented in this book are hypothetical and are for illustrative purposes only. They are not guarantees of results. Real estate markets, lending guidelines, interest rates, property values, rental income, and loan programs vary by location, lender, and time. Individual results will differ based on personal financial circumstances, market conditions, credit profiles, and property performance.

Readers should not make financial or investment decisions based solely on the information contained in this book. Before purchasing real estate, applying for a mortgage, or entering into any financial transaction, readers should consult with qualified professionals such as licensed mortgage brokers, real estate agents, financial advisors, accountants, and attorneys.

The author makes no representations or warranties regarding the accuracy, completeness, or suitability of the information contained herein and disclaims any liability for any loss, damage, or expense incurred as a result of the use or reliance upon the information in this book.

By reading this publication, the reader acknowledges and agrees that the author and publisher are not responsible for any financial decisions, investments, or outcomes resulting from the application of the information provided.

Risk Disclosure

Real estate investing and mortgage financing involve significant risk. While Debt Service Coverage Ratio (DSCR) loans can provide powerful opportunities for acquiring and scaling rental property portfolios, they also expose investors to financial, market, and operational risks. There is no guarantee that any real estate investment will generate positive cash flow, increase in value, or remain profitable over time.

Rental income may fluctuate due to vacancies, tenant turnover, economic conditions, changes in local rental demand, or property damage. Unexpected expenses such as repairs, maintenance, insurance increases, property tax adjustments, or regulatory changes may reduce or eliminate cash flow. DSCR loans are based on projected or current rental income, which may not continue at the same level in the future.

Interest rates, lending guidelines, and DSCR requirements can change at any time. Refinancing may not be available under the same terms, or at all. Some DSCR loans include prepayment penalties, adjustable interest rates, or balloon payments, which may affect long-term profitability and exit strategies.

Leverage amplifies both gains and losses. While DSCR loans allow investors to acquire more property using borrowed capital, they also increase financial exposure. A decline in property value, rent, or market conditions could result in negative equity, cash flow shortages, or foreclosure.

The author and publisher do not guarantee any financial results. All investment decisions should be made based on the reader's independent evaluation and consultation with qualified professionals. Readers assume full responsibility for any real estate, financing, or investment decisions they make.